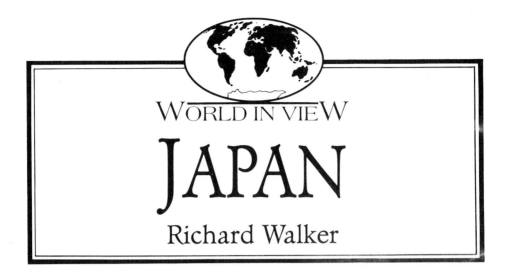

WORLD IN VIEW

JAPAN

Richard Walker

RSVP
RAINTREE
STECK-VAUGHN
P U B L I S H E R S
The Steck-Vaughn Company
Austin, Texas

Library of Congress Cataloging-in-Publication Data

Walker, Richard, 1961–
    Japan / Richard Walker.
        p.   cm.—(World in view)
    Includes index.
    Summary: Examines the geography, history, government, economy, culture, and people of the island nation of Japan.
    ISBN 0-8114-2457-X
    1. Japan—Juvenile literature. [1. Japan.] I. Title.
II. Series.
DS806.W25   1992
952—dc20   92-10766
                                                        CIP AC

Cover: *Mount Fuji and Lake Kawaguchi.*
Title page: *Itsuku-shima Shrine on the island of Miyajima*

Design by Julian Holland Publishing Ltd.

Typeset by Multifacit Graphics, Keyport, NJ
Printed and bound in the United States
by Lake Book, Melrose Park, IL
1 2 3 4 5 6 7 8 9 0 LB 98 97 96 95 94 93

Photographic credits
Cover: Tony Stone Worldwide; title page: Richard Walker; 5 Rick Siddle; 7 Richard Walker; 8 Nigel Blythe/Robert Harding Picture Library; 9 Frank Leather/Eye Ubiquitous; 12 Richard Walker; 13 Michael Boyd; 17, 18, 19 Richard Walker; 21 Rick Siddle; 23 Richard Walker; 25 The Mansell Collection; 26, 27, 32 Richard Walker; 35 Nigel Blythe/Robert Harding Picture Library; 37 Richard Walker; 40 Michael Boyd; 41 Richard Walker; 44 Robert Harding Picture Library; 46, 47 Michael Boyd; 50 Rick Siddle; 53, 56 Michael Boyd; 57 Richard Walker; 62, 63 Michael Boyd; 64 Rick Siddle; 65, 68 Michael Boyd; 69, 70 Rick Siddle; 72 Michael Boyd; 75 Richard Walker; 77 Nigel Blythe/Robert Harding; 78 Rick Siddle; 82 Michael Boyd; 84, 85 Richard Walker; 91 Robert Mcleod/Robert Harding Picture Library; 93 Richard Walker.

952
W

Contents

157867

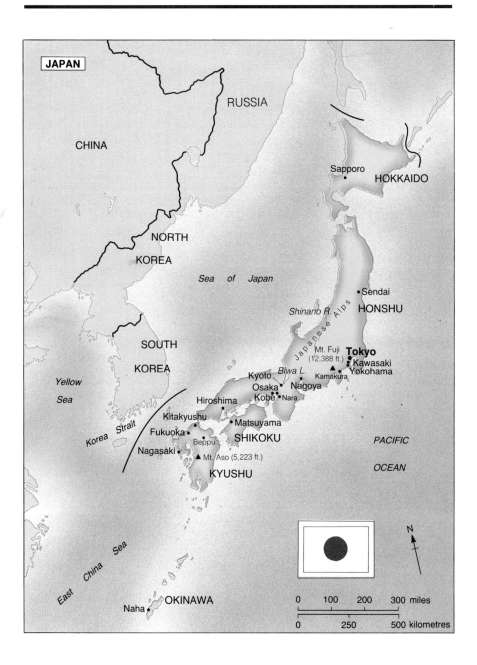

JAPAN

RUSSIA

CHINA

Sapporo

HOKKAIDO

NORTH
KOREA

Sea   of   Japan

Sendai

Shinano R.

HONSHU

SOUTH

KOREA

Mt. Fuji
(12,388 ft.)

Tokyo

Kawasaki

Yokohama

Yellow

Sea

Kyoto

Biwa L.

Osaka

Nagoya

Kamakura

Kobe

Nara

Hiroshima

Korea   Strait

Kitakyushu

Matsuyama

Fukuoka

Beppu

SHIKOKU

PACIFIC

Nagasaki

Mt. Aso (5,223 ft.)

OCEAN

KYUSHU

East   China   Sea

N

Naha

OKINAWA

0   100   200   300 miles

0   250   500 kilometres

1   An Island Nation

The country of Japan is made up of approximately 4,000 islands and islets lying off the east coast of Asia. To the north lies eastern Russia and to the west, the Korean Peninsula and China, separated from Japan by the Sea of Japan. To the east is the huge expanse of the Pacific Ocean. Japan's chain of islands extends more than 1,860 miles (3,000 kilometers) from tip to tip. This is the same distance as from Montreal in Canada to the warm sunshine of Miami, Florida. The four main islands, running from north to south, are Hokkaido, Honshu, Shikoku, and Kyushu, which together give the country its curved

The modern city of Shibuya during the rainy season. Like most Japanese cities, it is very crowded because there is little land available for building.

crescent shape. The largest of these is Honshu (which means "mainland") at 88,839 square miles (230,448 square kilometers). Tokyo, the capital of Japan, is on Honshu, in the middle of the crescent of islands. It lies on the same latitude as the Grand Canyon and the Rock of Gibraltar in Europe.

Japan's total land area is 145,834 square miles (377,708 square kilometers)—about the same size as California, or 50 percent larger than Britain. Yet, its estimated population of 123,770,000 is about half that of the United States and more than double that of Britain. It is not surprising that Japan has a very high population density, making it one of the world's most crowded places.

Mountains, lakes, and rivers
About 70 percent of Japan is mountainous, and much of this high land is forested. There are few large plains. Only 15 percent of the land is used for agriculture and a mere 3 percent for housing. In fact, 70 percent of the entire population lives on Honshu's southern strip of coastal plain, where Japan's major cities are situated. The scarcity of land available for housing means that it is very expensive. No land is wasted, and buildings are often built touching each other to save space. The Japanese Alps in central Honshu are the highest mountains in Japan, at 9,800 feet (3,000 meters) or more above sea level. Most of the other mountains in Japan are less than 6,500 feet (2,000 meters) high.

Most of Japan's lakes are in narrow valleys in the mountains, and so they are not very large. Biwa Lake in Honshu is the largest at 260 square miles (674 square kilometers). Because there is so

Earthquakes and Volcanoes

Japan lies in one of the earth's most active earthquake zones; hence earthquakes are quite common. Most are minor tremors that cause little damage, but severe earthquakes have killed many thousands. Today Japan is prepared for earthquakes. Gas and electricity are cut off immediately, and trains and elevators are stopped automatically. Skyscrapers are specially designed to sway and roll. In the last great earthquake in Tokyo, only 55 people were hurt.

There are more than 150 major volcanoes in Japan. Around 60 of these are still active, one of the most famous being Mount Aso on the island of Kyushu. After more than 80 million years, it still pours out huge clouds of steam continuously. The highest peak in Japan is the famous Mount Fuji, an inactive, or dormant, volcano. It is an almost perfect symmetrical shape and is often regarded as the symbol of Japan. It rises 12,388 feet (3,776 meters) and is especially beautiful in winter when its upper half is covered in snow.

Approximately 70 percent of Japan is mountainous, and much of it is forested. There are many active volcanoes, especially on Kyushu. Mount Aso, an active volcano, is situated in central Kyushu. It is a popular spot for tourists, who climb to the rim of the crater and bathe in one of the many hot springs that are nearby.

Symbols of Japan

No one knows exactly where the name *Japan* came from. It is said that it originated from "Jipangu," which the thirteenth-century Venetian traveler Marco Polo used after hearing the Chinese word for Japan. The Japanese themselves call their country *Nihon*, or *Nippon*, which means "land of the rising sun." The sun is represented in the national flag by a red circle surrounded by white.

The Japanese are proud of their nation. They have a national bird—the pheasant— which often appears in myths and legends. They also have two national flowers: the chrysanthemum, which represents the emperor, and the cherry blossom (*sakura*), which blooms all over Japan in spring.

The national anthem is called *Kimi ga yo wa*. The words come from an ancient poem more than 1,000 years old.

Cherry blossom parties, or hanami, *like this one are held all over the country when the cherry trees are in blossom. It is a tradition going back many hundreds of years.*

much high land, practically all the rivers are short and fast-flowing. The longest river is the Shinano, on Honshu, which is only 228 miles (367 kilometers) long.

From snow to sunshine

Japan has a warm climate, with four distinct seasons, as in the United States and most of Europe. However, the weather is different from region to region because it is such a long country north to south and also because of various ocean currents. This means that on any particular day there may be snow blizzards in the northern island of Hokkaido, cool conditions in Tokyo, mild and pleasant weather in Kyushu, and warm, sunny weather in Okinawa, one of the southern

Winter brings heavy snowfalls, blizzards, and freezing temperatures to the island of Hokkaido and the north of Honshu.

islands. Japan's average annual temperatures range from 43°F (6°C) in the north to 72°F (22°C) in the south.

It is not only between north and south that the climate varies. The range of mountains running down the middle of most of the country divides the Pacific side on the east from the Sea of Japan side on the west, and this also makes a difference in the climate. On the east side, winter days are often clear and dry, but on the west side, winter winds from Russia bring heavy snows. In the snowy areas, houses often have a door on an upper level, which is used when snow blocks the ground-level door. The capital, Tokyo, which lies on the Pacific side of Honshu, has a hot, humid summer, like most of the major cities of Japan, with the temperature reaching 91°F–95°F (33°C–35°C). The winter is cool or cold and generally dry, and the temperature may drop to 23°F (–5°C), although snow is unusual. The average throughout the year is a mild 59°F (15°C). On average it rains once a week, although much more during the rainy and typhoon seasons.

In areas other than the north of the country, the summer is long, hot, and humid. In early summer there is a rainy season, which lasts from June to mid-July. People wear plastic shoes and raincoats and carry umbrellas to protect them from the rain that pours down almost every day during this time. A typhoon season begins in late August and lasts six or seven weeks. All through this period typhoon winds batter the southwestern part of the country, causing a great deal of damage and sometimes even killing people. Elsewhere in Japan autumn is one of the best times of year, with pleasant temperatures and lots of sunny weather. The autumn colors of the leaves are particularly beautiful.

A country of trees
Because Japan stretches from the cool north to the warm south, it has a great many different kinds of flora and fauna. There are, for example, more than 1,000 different kinds of trees and shrubs. Many plants now grown in the United States originated in Japan.

The types of vegetation can be broadly divided into four zones. In the coldest zone, high up in the mountains, the vegetation is mainly small pine trees, birches, and heathers. A little lower, thick forests of both deciduous and evergreen trees cover the mountains. The next zone covers the moderately warm areas of Honshu, Shikoku, and Kyushu. The trees there are mainly evergreen and include a huge variety of firs. Pines, one of Japan's most popular trees and the subject of many paintings, can be seen everywhere. Other evergreens include the oak, the Japanese cypress, and the Japanese cedar, which grows to an impressive 128 feet (40 meters). There are also many deciduous trees, including several kinds of maple. The pine, the cherry, and the maple are Japan's most characteristic trees. The bright reds and yellows of maple leaves in autumn are enjoyed by people throughout the country. So is the cherry blossom, which blooms in a wave from north to south from mid-March to May.

Bamboo, another typical Japanese plant, ranges from bamboo grass to 48-foot-high (15-meter-high) giant bamboo forests. The stems of

The autumn reds of the maples make this garden in the temple of Shoren-in very beautiful. One of the quieter temples in Kyoto, its garden has not been changed for hundreds of years.

the giant bamboo have been used for centuries in many ways — for garden ornaments, vases, and gutters to channel water. South of Kyushu, on Okinawa, the vegetation becomes more tropical, and there are palms, sugarcane, mangrove forests, bananas, and pineapples.

Wildlife

The kinds of wildlife in Japan can be divided according to three areas. The first area covers the southern islands, including Okinawa; the second covers the north of Japan, which is mainly the island of Hokkaido. The third takes in Honshu and most of Kyushu and Shikoku. The third area makes up most of the country, and many of the animals there are similar to those in China and

Shika deer, native to Japan, are often seen near temples, shrines, or tourist sites, as here on the island of Itsuku-shima in western Japan. They are tame and enjoy being fed special biscuits that are sold nearby.

other parts of mainland Asia but are generally slightly smaller. There are some unusual species, such as the Japanese black bear found in Honshu. Here also are the Shika deer and the Japanese macaque, a red-faced monkey that lives farther north than any other monkey in the world. Honshu and Kyushu are home as well to a giant salamander that grows to 5 feet (1.5 meters).

The animals of Hokkaido in the north include the brown bear and the white-cheeked flying squirrel, which can glide through the air using special flaps of skin between its legs. In the southern islands, there are a few tropical animals and also tropical reptiles, snakes, and birds. Japan has over 400 different species of birds.

2   The Origins of Japan

There is evidence to suggest that people have lived in Japan for over 100,000 years, but the earliest civilization that we really know anything about was at a time called the Jomon period, between 8000 B.C. and 200 to 300 B.C. The *Jomon* people lived in caves and were hunters, fishers, and gatherers.

Eighteen thousand years ago, before the sea washed away parts of the land, Japan was still linked to the continent of Asia. Scientists believe it was at this time that Mongoloid people from Central Asia migrated to Japan and settled. The Mongoloid race forms one of the main racial divisions of mankind. They usually have yellowish skin and straight black hair. These earliest inhabitants spread throughout Japan, and later other Asian peoples from China, Korea, and Southeast Asia came and mingled with the earlier settlers. The blending gave rise to the modern Japanese people, who are a mixture of a number of Asian types. This can be seen in the many different facial features and skin colors of the people today. A small separate group called the Ainu live on the island of Hokkaido. No one knows where they came from, although it is thought that their ancestors may have been the original inhabitants of the country. Long ago they lived throughout northern Japan, but over the centuries they were slowly driven farther north as the settlers took over. The Ainu lived by hunting and fishing in the past, but today they live like everybody else.

Influences from China and Korea

In the early days China and Korea influenced Japan in many important ways. The first of these ways was the art of rice cultivation, which came from the Korean Peninsula in 200 B.C. and changed the Japanese way of life. Between the fifth and sixth centuries, various arts and crafts and agricultural methods came to Japan from Korea. So, too, did the Chinese writing system. This was a very important innovation because, until this time, the Japanese had no way of recording words. In the early sixth century the Chinese philosophy of Confucianism also reached Japan. Confucianism is a system of social organization that teaches respect for one's elders and loyalty, and it had a profound effect on Japanese society and ways of thinking. Also in the sixth century, Buddhism was introduced to Japan by way of Korea. However, it did not really begin to spread until the ninth and tenth centuries, when Japanese and Chinese monks began exchanging visits. During the seventh century, many Japanese scholars went to China to learn about life there and introduced new ideas to Japan when they returned. Many aspects of life in Japan, such as the style of buildings and various arts and crafts, were influenced by the Asian mainland in this way.

Growth of a ruling class

The social changes that took place led to the creation of different classes based on wealth. At the same time, ceremonies and customs began to develop, forming the beginning of the Japanese culture. Many small independent communities emerged, and these gradually united to form a single nation, headed by a large family, or clan, named Yamato. The Yamato clan had its own hereditary ruler, and this was the start of the imperial family of Japan.

During the fifth and sixth centuries, the emperors and the most powerful families ruled the country together. In the seventh century, Prince Shotoku began to build an ideal state based on the Buddhist principles of peace and salvation for everyone. When Shotoku died, his son was killed by an enemy family. But eventually the imperial family was established once more, and the emperors became even more powerful than before. They introduced a system under which farmers began to pay taxes on land the rulers had given them.

The first capital city

Before the year A.D. 710, Japan had no fixed capital. Instead it was moved as each new emperor came to the throne. In 710 the city of Nara became the first permanent capital. Over the next few years many Buddhist temples built under the guidance of the emperor Shomu flourished and became very powerful. The next two emperors felt the temples threatened their own power, and the capital was moved in 794 to present-day Kyoto. Kyoto was to be the capital for more than 1,000 years. The 400 years up to 1185 is called the Heian period. (Heian was the name of Kyoto at that time.) Toward the end of this time the Fujiwara family became extremely wealthy and powerful. Members of the family became prime ministers, and some of their daughters

Todaiji Temple in Nara, the ancient capital of Japan. It is the largest wooden building in the world and houses a huge bronze statue of Buddha.

even married into the imperial family. However, power went to their heads, and corruption grew. When civil war broke out in the middle of the twelfth century, they were overthrown. Another family, the Taira, came to power, but they too were overthrown by the Minamoto family.

The warrior rulers

During these years, the rulers found it more and more difficult to govern the outlying parts of the country, and so they began to employ warriors to control the peasants. These warriors were called *samurai*, and as time went on they became increasingly powerful. By the end of the twelfth century, they were more or less ruling the country. After the Taira clan was overthrown in

Even in the thirteenth century Japan was a wealthy nation, as the sumptuous interior of this temple in Kamakura shows.

1185, the head of the Minamoto family, a samurai by the name of Minamoto no Yoritomo, set up the first military government, or *bakufu,* in Kamakura, near present-day Tokyo. This marked the end of the Heian period and the beginning of the Kamakura period.

The head of the government was called the *shogun,* or military governor, and he let the various lords govern in their own localities. A feudal system was set up whereby these lords swore their absolute loyalty to the shogun, and the peasants had to give the same loyalty to their samurai overlord. Military outposts were set up throughout the country to collect taxes and to keep order. This style of military rule lasted for nearly 700 years.

The "wind from God"

During all this time, the emperor and his court remained in Kyoto, and although it was his official duty to appoint the shogun, he had become virtually powerless. Even so, a kind of tug-of-war went on between the imperial court in Kyoto and the military government in Kamakura.

Late in the thirteenth century the Mongols from Central Asia twice tried to invade the country. The second time they launched a huge fleet bearing 140,000 warriors, but luckily for the Japanese, a typhoon wrecked every single ship. The Japanese called this the "wind from God," or *kamikaze*, a word that was used again during World War II to describe Japanese pilots who flew suicide missions. Following this lucky escape there was unrest among the military, and the

Hiroshima Castle in the cherry blossom season. Typical of most castles in Japan, the inside is now a museum housing samurai warriors' armor and other weapons. The castle was destroyed and subsequently rebuilt.

emperor seized the opportunity to regain power for the imperial court.

Emperor Daigo II did not hold on to power for very long. He was driven into the mountains, and in 1336 a new military government was set up in Kyoto. However, bad administration and heavy taxes led to a number of civil wars in the years 1467 to 1568, with the warlords battling one another for control. The warlord Toyotomi Hideyoshi finally emerged as ruler of the country and remained so until his death. In 1600, when another warlord, Tokugawa Ieyasu, won a great battle and established his supremacy, it was the start of the Edo, or Tokugawa, era. In 1603 Tokugawa set up his military government in Edo, present-day Tokyo, and made himself shogun. As before, the emperor continued to live as a figurehead in Kyoto.

The Japanese language
Just where the Japanese language originated is not known, but it is similar in many ways to Korean, so the two languages may be historically related. Chinese has had a major influence on the language — more than 60 percent of all Japanese words came from China, and the Japanese also adopted the Chinese writing system.

In terms of the number of people who speak it, Japanese ranks sixth in the world (Chinese is first and English, second). For some people it is easy to learn to speak basic Japanese because the pronunciation and the grammar are straight-forward. The sentence order, however, is completely different from English. There are also different ways of speaking according to how old

Written Japanese is very complicated. It is made up of a mixture of kanji *(Chinese characters), two phonetic alphabets, and occasionally the Roman alphabet. However, it is versatile and can be written vertically, from top to bottom and right to left, or horizontally from left to right.*

you are, whether you are male or female, and how polite you have to be.

The most difficult thing about Japanese is learning to read and write. There are three different types of characters, as well as the Roman alphabet, which is occasionally used. Japanese is written in two ways. The traditional way is from top to bottom and from right to left, and this is the way most books, magazines, and newspapers are written. The other way is horizontally from left to right, as in English. This style is becoming more popular because it is easier to include numbers and foreign passages.

Many Japanese words have the same pronunciation but very different meanings. This is one of the reasons why the characters called

Japanese Characters

Kanji refers to the Chinese characters. There are about 50,000 different characters, or kanji in all, but only around 3,000 are generally used in Japanese, which includes approximately 1,000 kanji for names and places. Kanji are pictograms and were first used in China more than 3,000 years ago. For example, a simplified drawing of a tree represents just wood or one tree, two together represent a grove of trees, and three represent a forest. Most verbs, nouns, and adjectives are written in kanji.

Hiragana are added to the end of kanji to show the tense. There are 46 different hiragana, and each one corresponds to a single sound. Unlike the kanji, each hiragana by itself has no meaning.

Katakana are the third set. This set of 46 characters also corresponds to different sounds in the same way as the hiragana. These are used mainly to write words that have come from another language, most often English, and also foreign names and places. The hiragana and katakana are both uniquely Japanese and were invented in about the ninth century by simplifying various kanji.

kanji are still used — they make the meaning clear. At present between two and three million non-Japanese people are studying the language worldwide. This number is rapidly increasing as Japanese becomes more and more important internationally.

3 The Closing and Opening of Japan

In 1543 an important event occurred that had an enormous effect on Japan. A Portuguese ship was shipwrecked on an island in the south of Japan, and this marked the first contact of the Japanese with the West. The Portuguese sailors introduced many unfamiliar things to the Japanese, including guns.

Not long after this, traders and missionaries from Spain, Portugal, Britain, and Holland began to make regular trips to Japan. Trade also began with Thailand, the Philippines, and other Southeast Asian countries.

Japan closes its doors
The increasing number of foreign traders and Catholic missionaries coming to Japan began to worry the government. In 1639 the third shogun decided to stop all trade with the outside world and exclude all foreigners because he thought they and Catholic Christianity were a threat to the government. The only exception was the non-Catholic Dutch, but they were allowed to trade only on the island of Deshima in Nagasaki's harbor on the island of Kyushu. Once the doors were closed, the country isolated itself as much as possible. Japanese could not return to Japan from overseas, nor could they go overseas. Society became very rigid and repressive, and there were strict rules for the kinds of clothes people could wear, the kind of food they could eat, where they

Traditional samurai dress is worn by a man taking part in a local festival in Iwakuni, Honshu.

could live, and so on. Everybody had to obey the samurai leaders, and if they didn't, instant death was the likely penalty. Society was divided into four distinct classes with the samurai at the top, followed by the farmers, craftsmen, and merchants. This closed, feudal society continued for more than 200 years.

The opening of Japan
In 1853 four American warships under the command of Commodore Matthew C. Perry

Commodore Perry's expedition to Japan in 1853 showed the Japanese people many different aspects of Western life.

sailed into a Japanese harbor. Commodore Perry delivered a letter from U.S. president Millard Fillmore to the shogun suggesting that diplomatic relations be established between the two countries. The following year Japan and the United States signed a treaty that allowed U.S. ships to obtain fuel and supplies from two Japanese ports. Soon afterward, similar treaties were signed with Britain, Russia, France, and the Netherlands, and after a 200-year overseas trade embargo, trade finally resumed. At first there was strong resistance to opening the country, but as time went on more and more people felt that foreign trade and ideas were necessary in order for Japan to catch up with the West. A new government was needed, one that could absorb and adapt new ideas. In 1867 the new young emperor Mutsuhito and his nobles made it impossible for the last Tokugawa shogun to keep his power, and in 1868 the emperors took over once more. This event is known as the Meiji Restoration.

Rapid modernization

The Meiji era lasted from 1868 to 1912 and was a time of enormous change. Japan went from being an isolated and feudalistic country to one of the world's most powerful nations, with an army modeled on that of Germany and a navy modeled on that of Britain. Western ideas and cultures were adapted to suit the Japanese. This was done at a fast pace in an effort to modernize and strengthen the country. A Western-style parliament was set up, a constitution was written, and modern industries were promoted. Although the samurai class was abolished, the military remained powerful, and many samurai values remained a part of Japanese society.

To speed the process of modernization many Americans and Europeans were invited by the Japanese government to teach their skills, and between 1881 and 1898 nearly 3,000 Americans and over 6,000 British spent time in Japan.

Militarism

Now Japan's leaders wanted their country to be recognized among the world powers. Rapid expansion also meant that Japan needed more raw materials and markets for its industries. A sense of increasing pride in the new Japan and the continued strength of the army eventually led to wars with both China and Russia. They also led to the invasion of Korea, which was annexed by Japan in 1910. It was during this period that the Japanese government tried to edge out Buddhism and make Shinto the state religion, with the emperor at the top. People were encouraged to worship him as a living god in order to strengthen the feeling of national loyalty. The emperor from 1912 to 1926 was Emperor Yoshihito. Not much is known about his rule, but he is thought to have been mentally unstable. Emperor Hirohito succeeded him in 1926 at a time of worldwide economic depression that gave the military yet another chance to increase its power. In 1931 Japan invaded northeast China, and the next few years saw the invasion and conquest of other Asian countries.

World War II
By 1937, Japan had conquered eastern and central China and had started a campaign to drive Western powers from eastern Asia. The United States and Britain sent troops to support China. When Japan occupied Hainan Island in Indochina in 1939, the United States objected. It withdrew from earlier trade agreements and stopped sending oil to Japan. Japan then had to turn elsewhere for the oil and raw materials it needed. The plan was to capture the Philippines, Burma, Malaya, and the Dutch East Indies, where there was a large supply. During 1939, World War II started in Europe, and by 1941, when Germany was attacking Russia, all the European powers were involved. Japan took this opportunity to occupy Indochina. Japan also attacked Pearl

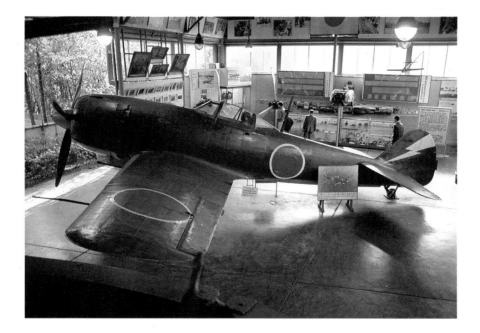

One of very few surviving Japanese fighter planes used in World War II. Most were destroyed after the end of the war, but a few, like this one, were discovered years later in shallow areas of bays or lakes.

Harbor in Hawaii and destroyed the U.S. fleet there. This brought Japan into the war, fighting mainly against the United States, but also against Britain and other Allied forces.

The early years of the war brought success to Japan. In 1942 the Japanese occupied Manila in the Philippines, the Dutch East Indies, and Rangoon in Burma. Then the U.S. Navy defeated the Japanese Navy at the Battle of Midway, an island in the Pacific. The United States and the other Allies gradually drove the Japanese back.

The end of the Pacific war came in August 1945. The Japanese had not replied to offers of a treaty, so the United States dropped the first atomic bomb on the city of Hiroshima, and three days later another atomic bomb was dropped on the

The Atomic Bomb Dome, Hiroshima. At 8:15 A.M. on August 6, 1945, an atomic bomb exploded almost directly above this building, destroying the city in an instant. The Atomic Bomb Dome ruin, as it is now known, is a memorial to the victims of the bomb.

city of Nagasaki. Both cities were almost completely destroyed. Japan surrendered on August 15, 1945.

A new start

Following Japan's defeat, the Allied forces, headed by the United States, occupied the country and set about its reorganization. A Western-style democracy was introduced, a new Constitution was written, and the armed forces were disbanded. In the new Constitution, which went into effect in 1947, power was placed in the hands of the people rather than the emperor, and war was forbidden. People were no longer encouraged to worship the emperor as a living god; instead, he officially became the symbol of

29

Heisei
Japan has its own way of counting the years. Each emperor's reign corresponds to an era, the first year being counted as year one. The present era started in 1989 (when Akihito first became emperor) as Heisei 1. Heisei 4 began on January 1, 1992.

the nation. He is now much like the monarch of Britain, without any real power but a very important figure in the minds of the people. Emperor Akihito, who was officially enthroned as emperor in November 1990, is the 125th to ascend to the Chrysanthemum Throne, as it is known in Japan. The Japanese imperial line is the oldest in the world.

The government
In the present system of government there is a parliament called the Diet, which is split into the House of Representatives and the House of Councillors. People over the age of 20 can vote in elections to select the members. As in Britain, there is a prime minister who is elected by the Diet members and who then forms a Cabinet. The Cabinet is changed on average once a year to give as many members as possible the chance to serve. Before World War II, only men could vote, but women were given the vote in 1945.

There are two main political parties in Japan: the right-wing Liberal Democratic Party, or LDP, and the Social Democratic Party of Japan, or SDPJ, a socialist party. There are also four smaller parties that are important. The LDP, which was formed in 1955 and has held power in the government ever since, has developed over the years very close links with business. This can sometimes give the impression that the country is run by a government/industry complex. The LDP is somewhat like a collection of different parties within one. There are five main groups, or factions, that continually compete with one another.

Recovery

It is a well-known fact that Japan is a highly advanced, industrialized country, but only 45 years ago, at the end of World War II, things were very different. There was a shortage of food, industrial plants had been destroyed, and cities lay in ruins.

After the war, Japan was occupied by the Allied powers, with the American General Douglas MacArthur in charge. The occupation had a twofold purpose — to ensure that Japan's armed

---

The Self-Defense Forces

War is forbidden under the Japanese Constitution, but since 1954 Japan has had a self-defense force. All of its members are volunteers. Like any other army, there is a ground force, a sea force, and an air force that together make up one of the world's most powerful military forces. It also has the third largest budget after the United States and the former Soviet Union. It keeps a fairly low profile in society because, although most people think it is necessary for the country's protection, the armed forces are not regarded highly these days.

Today Hiroshima is a modern, medium-sized city of a little over a million inhabitants. It is typical of modern cities in Japan and is the eleventh largest.

forces would not again become a danger to the world and to make the country more democratic, with a Japanese government that would protect individual rights. The Allied powers also helped Japan to recover by encouraging the development of its economy. The help given proved to be successful — within six years industry was back on its feet and has continued to grow rapidly. Today Japan's economy has become one of the largest in the world.

There were various reasons for such a dramatic recovery. The United States, as well as providing a lot of direct help, was a huge, open market for Japanese goods. Then, when the Korean War broke out in 1950, Japan was a very convenient supply and repair base for the Americans. This

Japanese Currency
Japanese currency is called the *yen*. There are coins of 1, 5, 10, 50, 100, and 500 yen, and notes of 1,000, 5,000, and 10,000. It costs about 300 yen for a cup of coffee (an expensive drink in Japan), 100 yen for a soft drink, and about 1,500 yen for a movie ticket. The Japanese economy is so strong today that the yen has become an important currency internationally. This means that foreign currency, such as dollars or pounds, will buy less in Japan than in other countries.

too helped Japan's economy. Also, the lack of armed forces meant that more money could be spent on rebuilding industries.

Another very important reason lies in the Japanese character itself — the willingness to put up with hardship and to work long and hard. This, together with the desire to catch up with the West, was a major force behind the rapid progress. During the 1950s and 1960s, Japan for the first time led the world in the production of radios, cameras, and home electronics, as well as pianos, trucks, and ships. Many of its industries continue to lead the world today. Japan is now an economic superpower. It plays a significant role in giving aid to poorer countries, and in the last few years the amount of aid has rapidly increased. In 1988 the amount of official aid given by Japan reached over 9 billion dollars. In addition, in the last few years Japanese overseas investment, which includes developing countries, has been the highest in the world.

4   A Mixture of Beliefs

There are 220 million religious people in Japan. This figure is almost double the real population and derives from the fact that most people consider themselves to be members of more than one faith. They are counted for each faith they follow, and this produces the artificially large religious population figure. Japanese people are traditionally tolerant of other religions and have tended to accept religions from other countries. Also they are usually not deeply religious, so they find it possible to believe in two or sometimes even three religions. In addition, religion in Japan is often concerned with practical day-to-day matters. Some occasions, such as weddings and funerals, are traditionally linked to certain religions.

Today there is no Japanese state religion, nor is there formal religious instruction at school. Nevertheless, the influence of religion on the Japanese way of life is very important.

Shinto
Shinto, which means the way or teaching of the gods, is Japan's native religion. In Shinto, people talk of the "eight million *kami*," or "eight million gods," because it is thought that every natural thing has its own god, or *kami*. Shinto has no founder and no official scriptures, such as the Bible, but it has a long history. It goes back to ancient times when the gods were invoked for protection from enemy tribes and for good harvests. Around the third or fourth century A.D., people began to build shrines at which to pray.

Later, Shinto was influenced by Buddhism and a Chinese philosophy called Confucianism, and several different types of Shinto arose. Then, a little more than 100 years ago, the government made Shinto into a state religion, encouraging everybody to worship the emperor as the most important Shinto god. This lasted until the end of World War II when Japan was defeated. The government was forced by the victorious Allied powers to separate Shinto from the state. The emperor made a public statement that he was not divine, and people stopped worshiping him.

Shrines still play an important part in people's lives. People visit them at New Year's; when a child is born; and to pray for just about anything — a safe journey, a good exam result, a successful romance, or even a raise at work. Many

Shinto, Japan's native religion, is in many ways practical. People will get a Shinto priest to bless the site of a new building, or even a new car, as pictured here. Many people also go to shrines to pray for a successful romance, a raise at work, and many other practical, day-to-day matters.

companies have a Shinto priest bless the site of a new office building before the foundation of the building is laid.

Most weddings in Japan are Shinto, conducted by a Shinto priest. Also, all shrines have their own festivals — usually once a year — and many people go to their local shrine at this time. Festivals are fun, with many stands near the shrine selling snacks and toys for children.

Buddhism

Buddhism has had a powerful influence on Japanese culture. Although there are only about 80 million registered Buddhists in Japan, nearly all Japanese people visit Buddhist temples. Funeral services in Japan are Buddhist, and after death, people are given Buddhist names. These names are kept at a special altar in the home.

Buddhism made its way to Japan from India by way of China and Korea in the sixth century. At the beginning of the seventh century the Japanese ruler was Prince Shotoku, who was a devout Buddhist. He ordered many temples to be built, including Horyuji Temple, which is now the oldest wooden building in the world. With the prince's help, Buddhism became the main religion of the aristocracy. About 600 years later, in the thirteenth century, a new kind of Buddhism evolved that was easier to understand, and it became very popular among the ordinary people. Zen Buddhism was part of this Buddhism. Since that time, Buddhism has become one of the main religions of the Japanese people.

In Buddhism, there is no God. According to Buddhism, people should try to reach the

This huge bronze statue of Buddha is just over 53 feet (16 meters) high. It dates from A.D. 752 and sits inside Todaiji Temple in Nara. The statue has been renovated several times. It is so large that several people can stand in the Buddha's palm.

ultimate state of self-enlightenment through meditation and deep thought. They should try to get rid of emotions such as hate and jealousy and replace them with love. Everyone should be tolerant and not fanatical about anything. Concepts and ideas like these affected architecture, medicine, and even farming techniques.

Zen Buddhism
About 9 million, or 11 percent, of Japanese Buddhists follow Zen. About 20,000 or one-quarter of all the temples in Japan are Zen temples.

In Zen, every aspect of life is important, even the most simple things, such as eating, sleeping, and walking. As in other types of Buddhism, enlightenment can be reached only by direct experience through the continued practice of sitting in silent meditation, or *zazen*.

There are two main types of Zen in Japan. One is called *Rinzai*. Its followers often meditate on strange riddles, such as the sound light makes when it falls on a leaf. In the past, this type of Zen was popular with the wealthy classes and the higher-up samurai.

The other main type of Zen is called *Soto*. This used to be popular among lower samurai and ordinary people because it taught that simply by devotion to zazen, anybody could attain enlightenment.

Zen has helped to shape Japanese culture and thought in many ways. The samurai spirit, the tea ceremony, Japanese flower arranging, and a good deal of painting and literature all reflect the influence of Zen.

Christianity

In 1549 the Catholic missionary Francis Xavier brought Christianity to Japan. The feudal lords of the time realized that contact with foreigners could lead to profitable trade, so they were friendly. The result was that by the last years of the sixteenth century, there were about 200,000 Japanese Catholics. Then the ruling powers decided that Christianity was becoming a threat. All foreign missionaries were ordered out of the country, and Christianity was banned on pain of death. In 1637 an uprising by thousands of Japanese Christians against the suppression of their faith was crushed, and nearly all the rebels were killed. Christians continued to be persecuted until 1873, but throughout those years believers went on practicing their faith in secret. After 1873, foreign missionaries were again allowed into Japan. Although they had little success in converting people to Christianity, they helped to introduce European and American culture. Today Christian values have become part of Japanese life, although less than 1 percent of the population is Christian. There are also many Christian schools and universities in Japan.

Festivals

Japan is a country of festivals, and almost every day there is a festival somewhere in the country. It may be one of the annual festivals celebrated nationwide, a famous regional festival, or just a small local festival. Some go back hundreds of years and are based on ancient rituals, and others are of fairly recent origin. Originally they were held to please the gods and to ensure plentiful harvests and prosperous communities. Today, however, most are simply occasions for fun and celebration.

Celebrating the New Year and spring

Of the main annual festivals, *Shogatsu*, or New Year's Day, is held over the first three days of the new year and is a time when hardly anyone

The Kimono

Today the vast majority of Japanese people wear Western clothing. Only in a few occupations, such as teachers of flower arranging or the tea ceremony, waitresses in Japanese restaurants, and bar hostesses, is a kimono the normal clothing. For other people, dressing up in a kimono is reserved for special occasions, such as New Year's, weddings, and coming-of-age ceremonies.

The kimono itself is a long garment that overlaps in front and is tied with a broad sash called an *obi*. Putting one on is difficult, and few people can do so without help.

Kimonos come in many different styles and patterns. Unmarried women wear colorful, long-sleeved kimonos, while the short-sleeved and generally plainer type is worn by married women. A man may also wear a kimono on very formal occasions, usually with a pleated, skirtlike garment over it. In the summer an informal cotton kimono called a *yukata* is often worn at home by both men and women. Many hotels provide yukata for their guests.

Although these women are wearing kimonos in the city streets, most Japanese women wear the kimono only on special occasions, such as weddings and New Year's. Few can put on a kimono without help.

At local festivals like this one in Iwakuni in western Japan, people often dress up in traditional costumes, making a very colorful parade.

works. Pine ornaments are put outside the front door to welcome the gods, and families pay New Year's visits to shrines and meet relatives and friends. Special dishes are prepared for people to eat at this time of year. Children receive gifts of money from their parents and relatives, and many Japanese women dress up in their traditional kimonos. Today people often take advantage of the holiday to travel in Japan or go abroad—skiing in the Japanese Alps is particularly popular.

Setsubun is held the day before the first day of spring. On this day, people traditionally open the doors of their houses and drive the demons (bad luck) out and call good luck in. They also visit shrines and temples. *Higan,* a Buddhist festival, also celebrates the coming of spring. It takes place around the spring and autumn equinox, that is, the time of year when day and night are the same length everywhere in the world. It is around March 21 and September 23. People visit their family graves and pray for the peace of their ancestors' souls.

Festivals for the dead and for the future

Another Buddhist festival, the Festival of Souls, or *Obon*, is celebrated in mid-July in Tokyo and in mid-August in the rest of Japan. The whole country is on the move at this time because everybody goes back to their hometowns. It is believed that at Obon the souls of the deceased return to visit, so people visit the family grave and place offerings on the family altar. All over the country, communities get together to hold outdoor dances. It is a lively and happy time.

In the autumn is *Shichi-go-san*, a Shinto festival, which literally means "seven-five-three." It is celebrated on November 15. Parents with 5-year-old boys, seven-year-old girls, and three-year-old boys or girls dress them up and take them to shrines, where they pray for a bright and happy future.

Christmas is not traditionally celebrated in Japan, nor is it a holiday. However, today many young people go to a party on Christmas Eve, and children receive presents and eat cakes. During the month of December, Christmas trees and decorations can be seen in all the shops up until December 25, when traditional Japanese New Year's decorations take their place.

5 Living in Japan

The standard of living in Japan is in many ways very high. Although, as in all countries, there are both extremely rich and extremely poor people, the vast majority of Japanese are fairly well off and seem happy with life in general. The divorce rate is much lower than in the United States and Europe, although it is increasing. There is almost no unemployment, inflation is low, and there is very little serious crime. Japan's average national income is one of the world's highest.

Social welfare

The Japanese government is steadily increasing its spending on social welfare. In 1988 a quarter of its total budget was spent on social programs. One issue that is becoming more and more important is social security for senior citizens. This is because Japan has the longest life expectancy in the world (75.9 years for men and 81.7 for women), and the proportion of older people in the population is rising fast.

There are two basic kinds of pension plans: private ones for company employees and a national plan for other people. Typically, after paying into the national plan for at least 20 years, people receive a pension when they reach age 60.

As with pensions, company employers contribute to a private health insurance plan, while everyone else pays into a national health insurance program. Most private plans cover from 90 to 100 percent of medical costs and around 70 percent of family members' costs,

Marriage

Weddings in Japan are usually Shinto. After the ceremony there is usually a formal reception when relatives and friends make speeches and sing songs. The bride typically changes costumes two or three times, ending with a Western-style wedding dress. Recently, church weddings have become quite popular, not for religious reasons, but simply because they are festive.

About seven couples out of ten marry as a result of meeting socially. The remaining three marry after having been formally introduced to each other in a uniquely Japanese custom called *omiai*. In omiai, a go-between, who is usually a family friend, arranges a meeting between the two, which the parents often attend as well. If the two get along well, they will probably decide to marry. In the past, most marriages came about through omiai.

In Japan people get married later than in most other countries. At present the average age is almost 29 for men and 26 for women. Couples also have fewer children these days, usually only one or two.

while the national program covers less. There are now so many people in the older age bracket that by the year 2000, 37 percent of the nation's total medical bill is expected to come from taking care of the elderly. In Japan there is no equivalent of the family doctor. Instead, many small hospitals attend to minor problems, and people go to larger hospitals for more serious matters.

The government has unemployment insurance for the unemployed, which at 2.6 percent of the population is very low compared with other countries. Depending on the length of time an employee worked before becoming unemployed, monthly payments of between 60 percent and 80 percent of the original wage are made for up to ten months.

Other forms of social welfare in Japan include programs for the handicapped and disabled and for environmental protection. In Japan, as elsewhere in the world, people are becoming more aware of the environment and how important it is to protect it.

Housing

An aspect of Japanese life that does not compare well with other countries is housing. Houses are both very expensive and much smaller than in the United States, Europe, or Australia, and backyards are tiny. At present just over 60 percent of homes are privately owned, but in the last few years, buying a house in an urban area has become almost impossible. Despite this problem, young people from rural areas are heading to the city in search of a more exciting life. This means that farming villages are in trouble because few

The lack of space for building in Japan means that lots are small, and buildings are often built almost touching each other.

young people are left to do the work. And those men who do decide to farm often find it very hard to find wives. Some end up marrying women from other Asian countries who come to Japan especially to find husbands.

Traditional Japanese houses are made of wood and have gray tiled roofs. In the cities, apartment buildings made of concrete are becoming more common. This is mainly because there is not enough space to build houses and also because apartments are convenient. Nevertheless, the apartments are often quite small.

Inside a Japanese house
The inside of a Japanese house is very different from one in the West. It has a small front entrance

One of the characteristic features of the inside of Japanese houses is the tatami *matting used in Japanese-style rooms. Nobody wears shoes when walking on these mats.*

hall, called the *genkan*, where families take off their shoes and put on slippers that are kept for themselves and guests. Shoes are never worn inside the home, partly to keep the floor clean and also to prevent damage to the flooring, which is not as durable as carpet.

The rooms have plaster walls and thick mats on the floor. These mats, called *tatami*, are made of rice straw covered with woven rushes. They measure just under 6 feet by 3 feet (2 meters by 1 meter) and are 4 inches (10 centimeters) thick. The size of rooms is measured by the number of mats, six or eight being typical even when the floor has no tatami mats. When walking on tatami, people wear socks, slippers, or go barefoot.

Most Japanese homes are a mixture of Japanese-style and Western-style rooms. In the Western-style rooms, including the kitchen, the furniture is much like that in the West. In the Japanese-style rooms people sit on cushions or legless chairs, and desks and tables are very low. One such table used during the winter is called a *kotatsu*, which has a built-in heater with a quilt that is laid over it to keep the heat in. A detachable tabletop is placed over the quilt. People tuck their legs under the table and wrap them in blankets to keep warm.

Everyone sleeps on the floor. A foldable mattress called a *futon*, used with a quilt, is the usual type of bedding. During the day, it is folded

---

Japanese Customs

Unlucky numbers—The numbers 4 and 9 are unlucky in Japanese. These numbers also mean death and suffering. Some hotels and hospitals do not have rooms numbered 4 or 9.

Bowing—When people meet or say goodbye to one another, they do not shake hands. Instead they bow, the depth of the bow showing the degree of respect. Bowing is not considered necessary between friends. Bowing is a custom that is taught at a very early age.

Seals—Rather than signing documents, Japanese people stamp them with a personal seal engraved with their name. Most people have more than one seal, and these seals are very important in everyday life. For example, withdrawing money from a bank or receiving registered mail requires a seal.

and put away so that the room can be used for other purposes. This kind of bedding is especially useful in a small house. Today beds are becoming popular, along with many other Western items.

Rooms are divided by sliding doors called *fusuma* and screens called *shoji*. Both have wooden frames with paper stretched across them. Shoji let light through, but fusuma do not.

Taking a bath in Japan is different from bathing in the United States and Europe. Bathrooms are similar to shower rooms — Japanese people thoroughly wash and rinse themselves outside the bath, then soak in a tub full of clean, hot water to relax.

Food and drink

The traditional Japanese meal is rice accompanied by various vegetables and fish, the main source of protein in the Japanese diet. Japanese rice is cooked so that the grains stick together, making it possible to be eaten with a pair of tapered sticks known as chopsticks. Japanese people use chopsticks rather than a knife, fork, and spoon. Restaurants use disposable chopsticks made of wood or sometimes bamboo. These are used only once and then thrown away.

In ancient times people used to eat meat, but they stopped with the rise of Buddhism, which teaches that it is wrong to kill. When the Meiji era started, people began to eat meat again, and today it is a normal part of the diet.

Soybeans are used a lot in Japanese cooking. Soy sauce is used as a dip and to flavor foods. *Tofu*, or soybean curd, is often eaten, and *miso*, or soybean paste, is also used to season many

Traditional Japanese food consists of rice and fish. Today people can also eat food from all over the world. Western food is especially popular. This food on display is called sushi. It is prepared to look very attractive, which is traditional in Japan.

dishes. Miso soup is part of the traditional Japanese breakfast. Edible seaweeds of many kinds are eaten, usually as an accompaniment to the main dish and to go with rice.

Since World War II, the Japanese diet has become more Westernized. Bread, milk, and other dairy products are now common. People can choose food from most other countries in the world, including American fast foods, which are especially popular among young people. Those people who have grown up eating Western food as well as Japanese food are considerably taller than people of past generations.

Few countries have as many restaurants as Japan. Eating places range from tiny snack bars or stands to extremely expensive restaurants serving delicacies from all over the world. Especially popular foreign dishes come from China, Korea, France, and Italy, although in most cases the food is changed slightly to suit the Japanese taste. The best-known Japanese dishes abroad are *sashimi, sushi, tempura,* and *sukiyaki.* Sashimi is raw fish served as a single course or as a snack. Only very fresh fish is used; it is dipped in soy sauce before being eaten and has a delicate taste. Sushi is rice cooked with vinegar and sugar, then made into patties and usually topped with raw fish. Tempura was brought to Japan by the Portuguese before the country's period of isolation. Vegetables or fish are coated with batter and then deep-fried for a short time. Like sashimi, the food is dipped in a special sauce before being eaten. Sukiyaki is cooked at the table in a casserole dish from which everyone serves himself. Tofu, Chinese cabbage, leeks, forest mushrooms, and beef are all cooked together, seasoned with soy sauce, and then dipped in a bowl of raw beaten egg before being eaten. Japanese rice wine, called *saké,* and beer are the most common drinks at mealtimes. At breakfast people usually drink green tea or coffee.

6 Education

The Japanese have always felt that education is important. The first schools were set up by the samurai class during the feudal age, which lasted until late in the nineteenth century. These samurai schools were all over the country and were only for the sons of the samurai. The children were taught cultural and moral subjects and martial arts to prepare them for their lives as samurai.

There was another kind of school for the nonsamurai classes, and in these schools, the basic skills of reading, writing, and arithmetic were taught to anybody who needed them. Both adults and children studied at these voluntary schools, and about 40 percent of the nonsamurai population actually made use of them. When the feudal times ended, compulsory education was introduced for the first time. In 1900 four years of education was compulsory beginning at age 6. In 1907 this was extended to six years, and many schools, colleges, and universities were founded thereafter. After the end of World War II, a completely new system of education was introduced by Americans, based on their own grade system. The education system has changed little since then.

The present system
Education in Japan today consists of nine years of compulsory education. Six years of elementary (primary) school from the ages of 6 to 12 are followed by three years of junior high school from

All schoolchildren wear uniforms, and many schools are strict about personal appearance. Some private universities and colleges also insist on uniforms.

the ages of 12 to 15. Senior high school lasts three years, from ages 15 to 18. University degrees usually take four years, but there are also junior colleges where students earn two-year degrees.

School is generally stricter and more formal than in the United States, Europe, or Australia. For both junior and senior high schools there are formal entrance ceremonies at the start, and graduation ceremonies at the end of the three-year courses. The school year begins in April after the spring break, which is usually about ten days long. The summer vacation is the longest, at around six weeks, and the winter break is about ten days, like the spring one. Everybody wears a uniform, and each student's personal appearance and hair length must be acceptable to the school.

English
English is taught beginning in junior high school and is a compulsory subject for the next six years. Anybody planning to go to college must pass an English exam. However, the exam does not usually test listening or speaking, which means that although many Japanese may be able to read and write English, few can speak well. This may improve soon because of a program that has recently begun to employ native English speakers to teach conversation in schools. At the moment, however, Japanese people who want to learn to speak English study at one of the many private English language schools that exist all over the country.

From Monday through Friday school is from about 9 A.M. to 3:30 P.M., with a midday lunch break. Saturday is also a school day, although only until midday. Students are expected to memorize many facts and to listen to the teacher rather than take part in discussions. The main aim of school is to prepare students for the many exams they will have to take. These are usually in a multiple-choice format.

Higher education
As a whole, the population of Japan is very well educated. There are hardly any people who cannot read and write, and a high proportion of people pursue higher education. Everybody finishes the compulsory nine years, and 94 out of every 100 go on to senior high school. After graduating, over 30 percent of those students go

on to college. This means that there are many colleges and universities, both public and private. Standards can vary greatly from one place to another.

There are about 130 national, or public, universities. The oldest and most famous is the University of Tokyo. Graduates of this university are guaranteed a top job with a big company. Among the more than 300 private universities, Waseda and Keio are the best known and, like the University of Tokyo, are very popular.

Challenging competition

Because graduating from a good university can help in getting a good job, there is strong competition to study at places like the University of Tokyo or Waseda. To get into any Japanese university, there is an entrance examination. Everybody who wants to go to a particular university takes the examination on the same day. It is generally harder to get into the public universities because they are often better as well as cheaper.

For many students, their whole school life is one big preparation for this exam at the age of 18. In order to stand a better chance of passing, most students also study at special private schools, called *juku*. After the ordinary school day is over, students head for their juku two or three times a week and often do not get home until late evening. Many students start going to juku at a very early age, some as early as 4 or 5. The best juku even have their own entrance exams, which may be as hard or even harder than the exams they are helping the students prepare for. Life is

These boys are on their way to a juku, or "cramming school." Almost all Japanese schoolchildren regularly go to a juku to increase their chances of getting into a good university. For some children the juku replaces compulsory school as the place where most learning takes place.

mostly study, especially in the year leading up to the exam, and students are under a lot of pressure to pass. For good students hoping to go to a top university like Tokyo, the courses they study at their juku are much more difficult than at their regular school, so school becomes a place to relax! Mothers take a very active role in organizing their children's education and sometimes may even attend the juku themselves in order to keep up and be able to coach their children at home. Education is considered to be so important throughout the country that there are between 100,000 and 200,000 juku, ranging from tiny one-room schools to huge juku chain corporations. It has become big business.

Juku do not just teach good students how to

All Work but Some Play

Although school life is hard in Japan, it is not all work. Occasionally there are special events, the most popular being the school trips in spring and autumn. In elementary school these are usually day trips to historical sites or zoos, but in the third year of junior and senior high school, such trips can last up to a week. Popular destinations are the cities of Kyoto and Nara, two ancient capitals of Japan where there are many famous temples and shrines. There are also trips to other parts of the country and sometimes even abroad.

Schools hold annual sports days, and students run festivals and put on plays. Various club activities include sports, music, and art.

Schoolchildren enjoying a trip to the ancient capital of Kyoto, the site of many of Japan's most famous temples and shrines.

pass the university entrance exams, however. They also offer lower-level courses for students who are having difficulty keeping up at school as well as many nonschool subjects, such as swimming, playing the piano, and learning to use the abacus. (An abacus is a simple counting machine using sliding beads supported by a frame. It was once widely used in Japan but has largely been replaced by the electronic calculator.) In addition, some students who have failed to pass the entrance exam study full-time at a juku in order to try again the following year.

After the examination
After all the hard work and effort of getting accepted to a university or college, the four years or so spent there are suprisingly easy by comparison. The breaks are long, and the homework is not excessive in many of the courses, especially the nonscientific ones. It is almost unheard of not to graduate successfully, so there is no fear of flunking out. There are lots of clubs that students can join if they want to, and the university or college provides its own affordable accommodations for students who are not living with their parents. Many students take part-time jobs to earn extra money.

7 Commerce, Industry, and Agriculture

Japan is a highly industrialized country with few natural resources, so it depends a great deal on imports of raw materials. Many of its industries are extremely successful, not only exporting manufactured goods to the rest of the world but setting up factories abroad. Over the last 40 or 50 years, Japan has gone from a situation in which almost half the work force was involved in agriculture and fishery to one in which fewer than one in ten workers is involved in farming. Well over half the working population is now in service industries such as banking and communications. Tokyo, along with New York and London, is now a world financial center. Its stock exchange is measured by the Nikkei Index.

Employment

In Japan the majority of people stay in the same company their entire working lives. Companies hire new staff every spring and usually recruit high school and college graduates. Most Japanese have a strong sense of belonging to their company — it is like being part of a big family, and the company looks after everybody until they either choose to leave (in the case of most women) or to retire at the age of about 60.

Length of service in a company is generally regarded as more important than ability, so an employee's salary goes up steadily year by year, and there is no fear of being fired or laid off. In

The Businessman
The typical Japanese businessman finds most of his time taken up with work-related events. A great deal of business entertaining is done in Japan, and socializing is also considered an important part of work. It is quite usual for a businessman to go out for a drink or meal with clients, colleagues, and sometimes the boss after leaving the office. Many companies organize regular events, such as annual company trips, end-of-year parties, New Year's parties, cherry blossom parties, and various athletic events. Within their companies, businessmen regularly change jobs. This can involve a transfer to another part of the country, or perhaps even abroad. In such cases, it is quite common for a married man to live away from his family, even if he is transferred abroad. This is because most people feel that moving children from school to school is detrimental to their education.

return for this security, people are very loyal to their company. Some even feel that it is more important than their real family. Also, the company takes an interest in their employees' private lives as well as work affairs. At weddings, for example, the boss is nearly always the guest of honor. This shows just how important the company is to Japanese people.

One of the drawbacks of the Japanese system based on length of service is that even if an employee is very talented, it is impossible for him or her to move up quickly. Partly because of this and partly because there are fewer younger and more older people than before, companies are beginning to reward ability rather than seniority.

Job-hopping is on the rise, although it is still rare.

In Japan many women work, but most of the top jobs are held by men, and in the majority of cases women act as assistants to their male colleagues. It is common for women to leave work after they marry, although more are choosing to continue working than before. The long hours that men spend working or with colleagues means that their wives usually have to take charge of the children's education and upbringing as well as managing the household. In most families the husband hands over his monthly salary to his wife, who then gives him his allowance and takes care of the rest.

Heavy industries
Japan's economic growth was built on its heavy industries, such as iron and steel. Japan's iron and steel industry is one of the world's largest. Nippon Steel, the largest steel company in the country, is the biggest in the world. The high cost of mining in Japan and the lack of mineral resources in general mean that iron and coal, used in the manufacture of steel, must be imported. Australia, India, and Brazil supply 80 percent of the iron ore, while 90 percent of the coal comes from Australia, Canada, and the United States.

The steel produced in Japan goes mainly to the flourishing industrial machinery, automobile, shipbuilding, construction, and electrical industries. Other metals are mined in Japan but are being imported more and more. This is because the metal ore that has been mined in Japan is of low quality and mining conditions are

Mount Fuji, with a chemical plant in the foreground. Japan's chemical industry is the third most important industry, its main product being sulfuric acid.

difficult. Also labor and energy costs are high, and the strength of the yen on the world market has made imported metals cheaper.

Much of the steel that is manufactured is used for shipbuilding. About half of all ships built throughout the world are made in Japan, which is now the world's foremost shipbuilder. Japan has held this position for around the last 30 years, after gaining a reputation for high quality and reliability. Recent years, however, have seen the rise of strong competition from other countries, especially South Korea.

The automobile industry

Steel is also the basis of the automobile industry. Japan is now famous for its cars, and since 1980

Japanese cars are famous throughout the world. Japan is the world's biggest automobile producer.

the country has been the number one automobile manufacturer in the world. It produces around 13 million vehicles each year of which about 10 million are passenger cars. Of the top three manufacturers in the world, two are Japanese — Toyota and Nissan — while General Motors of the United States is the other. Two other well-known Japanese companies, both of which produce over a million vehicles a year, are Mazda and Honda. Mitsubishi sells cars in 160 countries.

The automobile industry in Japan started many years later than in the United States and Europe, and at first Japan had to borrow technology from the West in an effort to catch up. Japanese cars rapidly became more sophisticated and gained a reputation for being both reliable and economical in their use of fuel. When rising oil prices in the 1970s made gasoline expensive, Japanese cars became even more popular abroad.

Recently, Japanese automobile factories have been built in other countries, not only to help meet the demand for cars but to reduce exports as well. Japan is also the world's leading producer and exporter of motorcycles, and as with cars, more and more are being made overseas.

Electronics

Japanese industry is probably most famous for its production of electrical and electronic goods. Many households throughout the world have at least one Japanese-made electrical product. Japanese companies lead the world in this field. Their use of the microchip has revolutionized the

Many Japanese companies that produce electrical and electronic goods are household names, and their products are sold all over the world. The most famous center for these goods is in Akihabara, in Tokyo, where all the very latest equipment is for sale.

watch and many other industries and helped develop an enormous variety of high-tech industries.

In 1986 Japan produced about 14 million televisions, 31 million video recorders, and more than 17 million cameras. In the last few years the Japanese market has expanded, as word processors, facsimile machines, and personal computers have become increasingly popular.

Agriculture

Until about 150 years ago, Japan was a farming nation. Today, because of rapid industrialization and modernization, only 2 percent of the nation's products are agricultural.

Although much of Japan's food has to be imported, one important exception is the

Small-scale rice cultivation is common in Japan. Very few farmers make a living from farming alone.

production of rice, the staple food, in which it is self-sufficient. Only 15 percent of the land is cultivated, and farms are tiny—approximately 3 acres (1.2 hectares) on average. As a result, farming methods are very intensive. Japanese farmers use larger quantities of fertilizer and artificial chemicals than any other country in the world, producing a very high yield for the amount of land available for farming. Their farms are also the most highly mechanized in the world.

The size of the farms makes it very difficult to earn a living through farming alone, so most farmers have another job. The government also helps them by buying their rice at an unusually high price and then reselling it to stores. This results in very expensive prices for rice. At present, the government does not allow cheaper foreign rice to be sold in Japan. There is pressure from abroad, mainly the United States, to open the market to foreign rice.

On Hokkaido agriculture is carried out more on a European scale, and products are similar to those in Europe. Farther south, tea and citrus

Forestry

In Japan, wood is the main material used to build traditional-style buildings and houses, so a very large supply of timber is needed. About half comes from Japan's own forests, and the rest is imported from countries such as the United States, Canada, and Russia. Most tropical wood is imported from Malaysia, the Philippines, and Papua New Guinea. At present Japan imports more timber than any other country.

fruits are grown, and in the southernmost islands tropical fruits are cultivated as well as fruits and vegetables similar to those grown in the southern United States.

Less than 2 percent of the land in Japan is good for grazing, so livestock farms are also tiny compared with those in other countries. Most of the good pasture land is on Hokkaido. The average beef cattle farmer has only 4 cows, and the average dairy farmer has approximately 30. Cattle feed is mostly imported, which means that beef is very expensive.

Farming is not a popular occupation among young people, who generally prefer more glamorous jobs in the city. For this reason, the future of the farming communities is uncertain.

Marine foods

Fish is a basic part of the Japanese diet. In fact, the Japanese catch and eat more fish than any other nation. Up to 150 years ago no one in Japan ate meat, so fish was the main source of protein. Mackerel, tuna, sole, sardine, cod, and squid are all caught and consumed in large quantities. At one time, whale meat was a traditional part of the Japanese diet, but it is now a less common food because of the ban on whaling for commercial purposes. Fish is also imported from various countries.

8 Transportation and Communications

One of the problems in such a densely populated country with thriving industries has been the need to create a good transportation network. Since the end of World War II in 1945, when hardly any of Japan's roads were paved, road construction and modernization have been going on at a rapid pace. Yet, the number of cars on the

Although Japan's road network has greatly improved, the sheer number of cars means that Japan has the most crowded roads in the world. On national holidays especially, long lines and traffic jams are very common.

roads has increased even faster, and with over 47 million registered vehicles, Japan has the most crowded roads in the world. Although road construction is difficult because of the many mountains, highways run most of the length of the country. However, there is a toll system for their upkeep, and motorists must pay to use them. Japan is one of the few countries where people drive on the left side of the road.

Because of Japan's extensive network of roads, most goods are transported by vans and trucks rather than by railroad. These vehicles account for more than a third of the total on the roads.

Rail transportation

In 1987 the Japan National Railways was privatized and split into six regional companies

During rush hour, all forms of public transportation are extremely crowded. In Tokyo, some lines are so busy at this time that special employees help squeeze passengers on the trains. Few people use cars to commute because of the crowded roads and lack of parking space. Tokyo's subway system carries 11 million passengers each day.

The Bullet Train

Japan's rail system is best known for its bullet train, or *shinkansen*, lines. These trains, which started operating in 1964, are very smooth and reach a maximum speed of 150 miles (240 kilometers) per hour. In their first twenty-five years of service, all the shinkansen trains together carried 2.1 billion passengers, traveling the equivalent of 20,000 times around the globe without a single major accident, a safety record that has never been equaled. It takes about six hours to get from Tokyo to Fukuoka in Kyushu, a distance of 731 miles (1,177 kilometers).

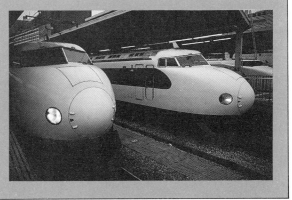

The shinkansen, *or bullet train, is one of the world's fastest and most reliable train services. It is rare for a train to be more than a few seconds late.*

plus a special company for the bullet train and several service companies, collectively called Japan Railways, or JR. These companies account for 80 percent of the almost 17,000 miles (27,000 kilometers) of railroads in Japan. The rest of the railroads are made up of private lines and subways, which are mostly in the big cities like Tokyo. Tokyo's subway system is the fourth largest in the world after New York, London, and

Paris, and carries millions of people each day.

The first railroad, which went from Tokyo to the nearby port of Yokohama, was built under the guidance of British engineers. It was just over 100 years before Japan's four main islands were linked by rail. The completion in 1988 of what was at the time the world's longest tunnel, a 33.5-mile (54-kilometer) tunnel between Honshu and Hokkaido, and also a very long bridge between Honshu and Shikoku made the last two connections.

Sea and air transportation

Shipping is important in Japan both for fishing and for trade. Japan imports very large amounts of raw materials, including oil, coal, timber, and metal ores, and exports equally large amounts of finished products. Japanese ships transport about 10 percent of the world's tonnage, including the country's own requirements.

Air transportation is important for a country that is situated off the edge of a huge landmass and bounded by the world's largest ocean. Japanese airplanes carry well over 46 million passengers a year. Many Japanese businesses are established in other countries, and in 1988 nearly 8.5 million passengers went abroad, a figure that increases each year. The principal airlines are Japan Airlines and All Nippon Airways.

Books and publishing

Partly because education is so important in Japan, the Japanese are enthusiastic readers. Books, magazines, and newspapers are all extremely popular. With over 4,000 publishers in Japan, publishing is big business. A lot of reading is done on trains traveling to and from work, and so pocket-size books are very common. A recent innovation is comic books for adults, which are often expressly designed to be read in the hour or so a reader spends commuting by train. There are countless comics, and they vary considerably in quality. Translation of foreign books, especially from the West, is big business, too, with about 3,000 titles being translated every year.

Newspapers

Nearly half the population reads a newspaper daily — more than in any other country. Every day in Japan about 60 million newspapers are

Reading is very popular in Japan, and there are approximately 4,000 publishers in the country. Many people read on the train while commuting to and from work or school. Newspapers and pocket-size books are popular among commuters.

published. Each newspaper is published in five regional editions.

Of the 124 national daily newspapers, the *Yomiuri Shimbun*, established in 1874, has the largest circulation at 13.5 million. In fact, this is the largest circulation of any newspaper in the world. In the United States the *Wall Street Journal* sells about 2 million newspapers a day, while the best-selling paper in Britain is the *Sun* at 3.9 million. There are also several national daily papers printed in English, the best known of which is the *Japan Times*.

Television

Television is extremely popular in Japan, and virtually every home in the country has at least one television set. People spend an average of three hours a day watching one or more of the six or seven channels.

Japan has a national station called NHK, which does not have any advertising. Instead it gets its money from a license fee that all television owners pay. NHK has two channels: one for educational programs and one for general programs. The commercial channels are all fairly similar, showing a variety of programs much like those seen in the United States or Europe. Broadcasting begins at 6 A.M. and continues to the early hours of the next day.

Many American and British films and news programs are broadcast both in English and Japanese. The newest television sets have a button for selecting English, Japanese, or both languages at once. Stereo broadcasts are also common.

Films

Television and the popularity of videos has meant that the number of people going to the movies is not as great as in the past. The movies' popularity was greatest in the late 1950s, declined in the 1960s and 1970s, and since the 1980s has remained fairly steady with an attendance of about 160 million a year.

Western films, especially American ones, are generally more popular than Japanese films and are shown in the original language with Japanese subtitles. Many Japanese films about gangsters and samurai are popular within the country. However, less conventional films are made, and some of these are successful abroad. The best-known Japanese film director internationally is a man named Akira Kurosawa. He first gained a reputation in 1951 when his film *Rashomon* won the *Grand Prix* at the Venice Film Festival. This film was followed by *Seven Samurai* and *The Throne of Blood* (based on Shakespeare's play *Macbeth*). In 1980 his film *Kagemusha* won the *Grand Prix* at the Cannes Festival. He released the film *Dreams* in 1990.

9 Sports and Leisure

Many people have an image of the Japanese as a nation of hard workers. It is true that they work longer hours than people in other industrialized countries, and in many cases, they put work before everything else. Only about half of all companies give two-day weekends, and the average paid vacation is 15 days a year. A great many people take only half of this because there is so much work to do and because it does not look good to take so much time off. Working overtime is accepted as normal.

However, leisure is becoming more and more important, especially for younger people. As in the West, simple pastimes like watching television, listening to music, reading, or going out for a drink or meal with friends are all very popular activities, but there are also Japanese

A popular activity in Japan is singing in public. Many amateur singers go to karaoke *bars or even to parks where they can practice singing. They always have a good audience.*

National Holidays
There are 13 national holidays in Japan. On these days, schools, companies, and government offices close, but many stores and restaurants remain open.

New Year's Day—January 1.
Adult's Day—January 15. Ceremonies all over the country celebrate those who reach the age of twenty that year and legally become adults.
National Foundation Day—February 11. Legend says Jimmu Tenno, the first emperor of Japan, came to the imperial throne on this day in 660 B.C.
Vernal Equinox Day—March 1. A Buddhist festival for nature and all living things.
Greenery Day—April 29. Marked Emperor Hirohito's (Showa's) birthday until his death in January 1989. Now a day for nature, reflecting his love of trees and plants.
Constitution Day—May 3. Commemorates the Japanese Constitution, which came into effect in 1947.
Children's Day—May 5. Parents pray for the happiness of their children, and mothers are thanked for their work.
Respect for the Aged Day—September 15. To show respect for the elderly with gifts and entertainment.
Autumnal Equinox Day—September 23. A Buddhist festival day to remember ancestors and visit the family grave.
Sports Day—October 10. Sporting events held for all ages on the date the 1964 Tokyo Olympics started.
Culture Day—November 3. Cultural activities take place all over the country.
Labor Thanksgiving Day—November 23.
Emperor's Birthday—December 24. Emperor Akihito was born in 1933.

ways of spending leisure time. *Pachinko*, a pinball game, is extremely popular, especially with men. Pachinko parlors are everywhere in Japan, instantly recognizable by their bright, flashing neon lights, and people who play well often win quite a bit of money. Another Japanese leisure activity that has become popular is *karaoke*. Karaoke bars first appeared about 15 years ago. Patrons use the microphones provided to sing along to popular songs. Some people even have karaoke machines in their own homes. The karaoke craze has spread around the world.

Sumo wrestling is becoming popular in countries other than Japan. The few top wrestlers are national heroes.

Sumo

A variety of sports are leisure activities in Japan, but *sumo* is the most traditional. Sumo is a uniquely Japanese sport that goes back to ancient

times. It started, not as a sport, but as a ritual connected with prayers for a good harvest and developed into a spectator sport in about the sixth century. Much of the ancient ritual still exists in the modern sumo that is so popular today. Two wrestlers, dressed in loincloths, face each other in a ring that is about 15 feet (4.7 meters) across. First they do several warm-up exercises and rituals, such as throwing salt onto the ring to purify it. Then they touch their fists on the ground and charge at each other. The first wrestler to be pushed out of the ring or touch any part of it except with his feet loses. Being big and heavy is an advantage, so most wrestlers eat a special sumo diet to gain as much weight as possible. Weight alone is not enough, however. Hard physical training is also essential to build the

This is a golf driving range in the city of Shinjuku. Golf is a very popular sport in Japan.

Other Popular Sports

Golf has gone from being a "rich person's game" to one that is enjoyed by many business people. There are now about 1,500 courses in Japan, but most courses are private, and it is still a very expensive sport. As in the West, the game is often used for business socializing. However, it is becoming increasingly more popular as just a hobby, especially among young women. Professional golf tournaments are now major events in Japan, and several Japanese golfers are well known internationally.

Tennis, like golf, has become extremely popular in the last 15 or 20 years, and there are so many players that it can be difficult to get a court. It is not as expensive as golf and so is more favored by students and younger people in general. The major international tennis tournaments are broadcast live on television, and more and more famous tennis players are coming to Japan to play.

Fishing is a hobby enjoyed by many Japanese. This is not surprising considering Japan's many lakes and rivers and its long history as an island fishing nation. About 20 years ago fishing began to gain popularity, and now about 15 million people enjoy fishing as a hobby.

strength necessary to win a sumo tournament.

A sumo tournament lasts 15 days, with each wrestler fighting once each day. The person with the fewest losses wins the tournament. There are six tournaments a year, three in Tokyo and three elsewhere in the country, and on the basis of each wrestler's performance his rank is decided. The top rank is called *yokozuna*. In the past 300 years only 60 wrestlers have been given this title. Sumo tournaments are broadcast on television and radio, and are followed by many people, including foreigners. In fact, there are one or two good non-Japanese wrestlers from Hawaii. Sumo is also practiced as an amateur sport in schools and universities.

Baseball

Introduced by Americans in 1873, baseball is without a doubt the most popular sport in Japan. Professional baseball began in 1934 and became especially popular after World War II. There are two leagues, the Central League and the Pacific League, each with six teams. The two winners play each other in an annual event known as the Japan Series.

Amateur baseball is also very popular, and the All Japan High School Baseball Championship, the top amateur event, is held each summer. It is watched and enjoyed by people all over the country. As many as 3,900 schools take part. To play in the winning team is every Japanese schoolboy's dream.

The martial arts

The best-known martial arts are *judo, karate, kendo* (or Japanese fencing), *kyudo* (or Japanese archery), and *aikido*. Originally, they were more than just sports because mental training and discipline were considered to be as important as physical training and skill, but today the physical side is emphasized. In all the martial arts there are different ranks that depend on skill. To reach the top rank is extremely difficult and usually takes many years.

The "way of softness"
Judo, karate, and aikido are performed without weapons. *Karate* means "empty hand" in Japanese because no weapons other than the body are used. It started in China about 1,300 years ago and first came to Japan in the fourteenth century by way of the southern island of Okinawa. It is a system of unarmed combat that uses precise blows and kicks to the body to defeat the opponent.

During contests, accuracy, timing, and correctness of posture are all extremely important. In addition, one's *kiai*, or attacking shout, is vital because it is a sign of mental concentration. There are over 23 million karate enthusiasts worldwide.

Judo means "the way of softness" because it is mainly defensive and requires skill rather than just strength. Modern judo started a little over 1,000 years ago, developing from more traditional martial arts. Its aim is to train both the body and mind. Two contestants, each wearing a jacket, trousers, and belt, try to throw each other to the ground within an area measuring about 30 square feet (9 square meters).

Since the 1964 Tokyo Olympics, judo has been an Olympic sport and is so popular that around 5 million people are practicing the sport worldwide. In Japan it is taught in schools.

Aikido is a little like judo but only teaches

The Japanese are very enthusiastic photographers. When they visit monuments in Japan or abroad, they are eager to keep a photographic record.

people how to defend themselves, not how to attack and defeat their opponents. The aim of aikido is to train the mind as well as the body. Aikido has a much shorter history than the other martial arts since it only started in the 1920s.

Using weapons

The Japanese have also developed many skills using weapons, such as swords or bows and arrows. These skills are still taught both in Japan and many other countries.

Kendo is a type of fencing in which the contestants use bamboo swords and wear special protective clothing. It has been an international sport since 1970 and is practiced in both junior and senior high school. In ancient Japan, being able to use a sword skillfully was essential for the samurai, and they developed the martial art of kendo over the years. Although this kind of fencing is mainly practiced as a sport, in the past, moral training was part of learning kendo.

Kyudo, or Japanese archery, also has not changed very much from its original form. Long ago, before the introduction of firearms, the bow was an important weapon used for fighting and hunting. Learning to use it well was a necessity. The bow itself is made of a mixture of bamboo and other woods and is over 6 feet (2 meters) long.

Sightseeing

In many places in Japan there are numerous attractions that people like to visit on day trips and longer vacations. Throughout Japan there are picturesque mountains, highlands, and lakes. There are also beautiful places on the coast, especially beside the Sea of Japan where it is much quieter than on the Pacific side. In southwestern Honshu near Hiroshima is the Inland Sea, where there are countless small islands, some too small to live on. It is a good place to go sailing because all the islands make the sea very calm. A number of these places have been made into national parks. Matsushima Bay on the Pacific coast of northern Honshu is also a national park. Here the sea flooded an area of volcanic hills, leaving numerous islands that have been eroded to form cliffs, caves, and tunnels. The semitropical island of Okinawa, almost 1,000 miles (1,600 kilometers) south of Tokyo, has some beautiful beaches and coral reefs. People often go there for a seaside vacation.

The town of Beppu in Kyushu is famous for its many hot springs. Some are used to bathe in. Others, not used for bathing, are called "The Hells," one of which is shown here.

Hot and cold

One of the most popular things to do is to go to a hot spring to relax. There are thousands of hot springs in Japan, since it is a volcanic region. A day or two spent relaxing at a hot spring is often combined with a stay at a Japanese-style inn, where visitors sleep on tatami mats on the floor. More than 3,500 hot springs and geysers are to be found in Beppu in northeastern Kyushu. The town has become a popular spa where people go for medical treatment.

The island of Hokkaido has wide plains and tall mountains and is a good place for skiing in the winter. A famous ice festival is held every winter in the city of Sapporo. People from many different countries make ice sculptures—

84

The view of the Seto Naikai, *or Inland Sea, seen from the summit of the island of Itsuku-shima, near Hiroshima. The Seto Naikai is bordered by southwest Honshu and the island of Shikoku and is an area of countless small islands and calm sea.*

Overseas Travel

Every year more and more Japanese are going abroad for their vacations. Although the image of groups of middle-aged people carrying cameras and hurrying from place to place is often not far from the truth, individual travel, especially among young people, is on the rise. Most people can only take short vacations, usually a maximum period of a week to ten days.

The United States, Taiwan, South Korea, Europe, and Hong Kong are all favorite destinations. By far the most popular place in the United States is the island of Hawaii. In Europe, Britain, France, and Germany are the countries most Japanese want to visit.

85

sometimes as big as houses — and display them in the center of the city.

Other attractions range from cultural centers like Kyoto and Nara to amusement parks, the best-known being Tokyo's Disneyland. There are also several famous Japanese gardens for visitors to enjoy.

10 Art and Culture

In both work and leisure, the Japanese like to do everything well. They take pleasure in artistic pursuits, such as flower arranging and painting, and they enjoy music and the theater in all its forms. Many of their ideas have been adopted by the West.

The tea ceremony

The Japanese love tea. Japanese tea is green and is served without milk or sugar. There is a special kind of powdered tea that turns bright green and is bitter-tasting when mixed with hot water. It is this kind of tea that is used in the tea ceremony, or *sado*. Sado first came to Japan from China about 1,200 years ago and became popular about 500 years later. It was refined in the sixteenth century by a man called Sen no Rikyu with the help of the shogun of the time. Sen no Rikyu came to an unfortunate end when, in 1591, he argued with the shogun and was forced to commit *seppuku*, a ritualistic and honorable form of suicide.

Sado is a popular hobby among young women and some men, and the ceremony usually takes place in a small room overlooking a Japanese-style garden. A special etiquette surrounds the serving and drinking of the tea. The host carefully prepares the room beforehand, then makes and serves the tea in a special way. The guests receive and drink it also in a special way, being careful to show their appreciation. The relationship between the host and guests is very important.

Taming nature

Ikebana, or Japanese flower arranging, goes back about 400 years. In the past, both the tea ceremony and ikebana were studied by young women before marriage, but today they are simply popular hobbies.

In traditional ikebana, natural flowers and twigs are artistically arranged to look as natural as possible. Sometimes the different parts represent the sky, the earth, and the moon, and are arranged accordingly. Recently, new styles of ikebana have emerged in which man-made materials such as iron or plastic are used, and the usual traditions are not followed. Altogether, there are nearly 3,000 styles that people can study in Japan.

Bonsai, or the art of cultivating miniature potted trees, is Japanese in origin. The seed of a normal tree is planted, and as it starts to grow, it is repotted regularly. Each time the roots are carefully trimmed to slow its growth. Fast-growing shoots are cut off, while suitable ones are protected. Just about everything concerning the tree's growth is controlled, including the shape of the trunk and the shape and position of the roots. The result is a tiny tree with a shape very pleasing to the eye.

Bonsai trees last much longer than other potted plants, some up to 100 years or more. The type of tree most commonly used is the pine, but many other kinds are also used.

Calligraphy

Calligraphy, the art of handwriting, exists in the West as well as in Japan. However, it is more highly developed in countries like China, Korea, and Japan, where people write in kanji. Kanji give greater scope for different styles of writing because they are more complicated to write than letters. Also there are many kanji to choose from, each having a different meaning.

There are three basic styles of calligraphy, all of which use black ink and brushes of various sizes. As with many things in Japan, the origins of the art lie in China. Calligraphy came to Japan in the eighth century, and over the years uniquely Japanese styles were developed. Today it is a popular hobby with many people.

Painting

Japanese painting has a special style that began about 1,000 years ago. It started with a Chinese style of the time to which Japanese ideas were added. In the sixteenth century some painters employed by the shoguns painted directly on sliding doors and folding screens. They are now known as the Kano School of painters.

Probably the Japanese paintings best known in the West are those of the Edo era in the eighteenth and nineteenth centuries. These paintings are called *ukiyo-e*. Many of them are color prints made from carved wood blocks. They cover many themes: the theater, young women, sumo wrestlers, and landscapes. A particularly famous landscape painter was Hokusai, who painted a series of 36 views of Mount Fuji in the nineteenth century. Western art was introduced not long after this by the Dutch, and it soon became popular. Today art schools usually teach Western-style art.

Swordsmiths

Japanese swordsmiths were master craftsmen. The Japanese sword with its razor-sharp edge and gleaming curved blade is a work of art. As long as 1,200 years ago swords were being made in Japan, but in the thirteenth century when the samurai were becoming powerful, swords were improved to suit them.

Right up to the sixteenth century, when firearms first appeared, swords were the main weapons for fighting. They became the symbol of the warrior because only the samurai were allowed to wear them.

Particularly good ones were treated with the utmost care and passed on from generation to generation, always looking brand new.

With the Meiji Restoration of 1867–68, the samurai were banned from wearing the swords, and most of the good ones ended up in museums and private collections.

Japanese theater

Noh, kabuki, and *bunraku* are the names of three kinds of uniquely Japanese traditional theater entertainments. Each kind has its followers, but most Japanese seldom go to performances, partly because there are few traditional theaters.

Noh is the oldest form of theater in Japan, dating from the fourteenth century. It is a kind of dance-drama in which the actors often wear masks. The actors themselves move slowly and in very stylized ways to the accompaniment of drums and flutes. There is no real script, only a narrative of chants and songs sung by a chorus, and very few props on the stage. The

Japanese theater has a long tradition, but there are also more modern plays.

approximately 250 Noh plays, which were originally for the entertainment of the samurai, are divided into five groups of plays about gods, samurai, women, madness, and demons.

Kabuki

Kabuki is the most popular traditional theater form and dates back about 300 years. Like Noh, the actors' movements are stylized, and they speak in a set way with a special rhythm. The music and dancing are important to the performance, and the music is usually played on several three-stringed Japanese lutes, called *shamisen*, along with other Japanese instruments. There is a revolving stage that is used for quick scene changes. The actors are all very quick to change costumes and can become completely different characters in a matter of seconds. There are both male and female characters in the plays, but today all the parts are played by men. In the very first kabuki performances, women played men, and men played women. The art of kabuki acting is passed on from father to son, and training begins at a very early age. The actors themselves are considered to be very important, and the play is often changed to suit the talents of a particular actor.

Bunraku
Japanese puppet theater, or bunraku, first became popular in the seventeenth century. The puppets, which are about 4 feet (1.2 meters) tall, can weight up to 22 pounds, are very carefully made, and are dressed in beautiful costumes. Three people, who wear black so as not to be seen against the dark background, operate a single puppet and bring it to life. One person operates the head and one arm, another operates the other hand, and the third operates the feet or, if the puppet represents a woman, moves the skirt to make it look as though the puppet is walking. These people study for many years and are very skilled. The story, which is usually about love or war, is chanted to the accompaniment of shamisen music.

Traditional music
Western-style rock, pop, jazz, and classical music are as popular in Japan as they are in the United States and Europe. It is the kind of music that most people enjoy. There are also several types of

traditional Japanese music, which use a five-note scale, unlike Western music, which typically uses seven notes. The oldest music of this kind, which came from China and Korea, is that used for imperial ceremonies. Another kind is music played on the *biwa*, a kind of short lute. This usually accompanies a long ballad, often about famous samurai's heroic deeds, or great battles.

Koto music is more recent, going back about 300 years. The koto is a thirteen-stringed Japanese harp. The koto played alone, or with two other Japanese instruments, the shamisen and a bamboo clarinet called a *shakuhachi*, is the kind of music that is thought of as typically Japanese. The koto is a popular instrument to learn to play, especially among women.

One kind of music is played just on the

Traditional musicians inside Izumo shrine in western Japan are taking part in the New Year celebrations.

shakuhachi. Long ago, this instrument was played by Buddhist monks who spent their time wandering from place to place. The monks wore large straw hats that completely covered their faces, and because of this, it was a common disguise for samurai who had done something wrong and were on the run.

Index

© Heinemann Children's Reference 1992
This edition originally published 1992 by
Heinemann Children's Reference, a division
of Heinemann Educational Books, Ltd.